The RE Teacher's SURVIVAL Guide

Text copyright © Jane Brooke 2014
Illustrations copyright © Gemma Hastilow 2014
The author asserts the moral right to be identified as the author of this work

Published by
The Bible Reading Fellowship
15 The Chambers, Vineyard
Abingdon OX14 3FE
United Kingdom
Tel: +44 (0)1865 319700
Email: enquiries@brf.org.uk
Website: www.brf.org.uk
BRF is a Registered Charity

ISBN 978 0 85746 220 6

First published 2014
10 9 8 7 6 5 4 3 2 1 0
All rights reserved

Acknowledgements
Enquiry Model by Ian Patience, adapted from the work of Lois Hetland and Kimberly Sheridan,
used with permission.

Cover illustration: © Gemma Hastilow/Beehive

Every effort has been made to trace and contact copyright owners for material used in this
resource. We apologise for any inadvertent omissions or errors, and would ask those concerned
to contact us so that full acknowledgement can be made in the future.

A catalogue record for this book is available from the British Library

Printed and bound by CPI Group (UK) Ltd, Croydon CR0 4YY

The RE Teacher's SURVIVAL Guide

A practical guide to teaching RE in primary schools

Jane Brooke

Read the quotations from children throughout the book and hear what excites them most about RE.

Contents

✳

Introduction

'RE is my favourite subject,' a primary school teacher said enthusiastically. When asked why, she explained that the children have more time to discuss, enquire and explore in RE than in other areas of the curriculum. Many teachers, though, do not feel quite so positive when faced with the whole curriculum that must be taught. Their comment is more likely to be, 'Not RE *as well*?'

However, once we have gone beyond the idea that RE is about hearing a story, filling in a worksheet and colouring in, we begin to realise that it is a subject in which children are free to reason and to give their own opinions on beliefs that are of great importance to much of humanity, such as 'Is there life after death?' or 'Does God exist?'

This book sets out to help a new RE teacher or subject leader with practical approaches. It provides a starting-point for all that a teacher needs, not only to survive in RE but to inspire and be inspired in RE.

So, draw a breath… RE could become the most exciting subject that you teach!

*

What do I need in my survival kit to teach RE?

The answers to the questions below will fill the survival kit very well! These are the main chapters covered in this book.

- What do I teach in RE?
- What are the top tips for a new RE teacher?
- How do I plan RE?
- Can you give an example of a good learning cycle for RE?
- What is enquiry-based learning?
- How important are learning objectives in RE?
- What should be in an RE policy document?
- How do I create a variety of approaches to learning?
- What about visits and visitors?
- How do I use religious artefacts?
- How do I respond to difficult questions?
- What mistakes might I make?
- How do I assess RE?
- What do I need to do as a subject leader in RE?

The book also contains appendices with the following aids to teaching.

- What does the law say about RE?
- Connecting Spiritual, Moral, Social and Cultural education with RE
- A sample lesson observation form
- More about the solid–liquid–gas analogy in enquiry learning
- References and sources

1. What do I teach in RE?

In **community schools**, teachers follow the locally agreed syllabus. The Standing Advisory Committee on Religious Education (SACRE) appoints a group of people, called an Agreed Syllabus Conference, to write the syllabus. Some local authorities adopt a syllabus from a neighbouring authority. In **Voluntary Aided church schools**, the governing body can choose which syllabus to follow and may choose the locally agreed syllabus, the diocesan syllabus or any other syllabus. **Academies** follow the syllabus according to their funding agreement, and **Free Schools** may choose. Some local authorities provide schemes of work to accompany the syllabus.

> ❓ **What if…?**
> What if I don't have enough time allocated to teach RE?
>
> ☺ **Answer from a teacher**
> The Agreed Syllabus usually states the recommended time required to deliver the syllabus. The school should allow that amount of time. If time is still insufficient, try to use RE learning objectives to deliver other areas of the curriculum. For instance, I have taught the story of Daniel in art, using clay to represent Daniel's thoughts and feelings for each part of the story.

? What if…?

What if Buddhism is on the syllabus and I don't know anything about it?

☺ Answer from a teacher

When I had to teach Buddhism, I read around it using a GCSE textbook to help me. Then I thought about how to make it accessible to my pupils, just as I would any other subject. I started by thinking about 'change' around the world and in the world, so that the children absorbed the idea of everything changing and the concept of impermanence.

*

2. Top tips for a new RE teacher

1. Ask your school RE subject leader to go through the RE plans and programmes of study with you.
2. Find out how often assessment takes place and ask for some previous examples.
3. Read the RE policy in your school with the RE subject leader.
4. Check how much written work is absolutely necessary. Discussion, quizzes, artwork, music and drama are also valid ways of consolidating RE. There may be opportunities for cross-curricular work. Use art, poetry and music to teach the RE learning objectives.
5. Familiarise yourself with the school RE resources. Check that texts are not out of date. Explore RE websites and look at YouTube (www.youtube.com) and TrueTube (www.truetube. co.uk).
6. Ensure that you keep your world faith knowledge up to date by reading, visits, interviews and so on.
7. If you discover unfamiliar words, check how to pronounce them with the subject leader, parents, local faith leaders or the internet. Words often vary according to local dialect.
8. When talking about religions with children, preface statements with 'Christians believe…' or 'Some Christians believe…' or 'Some Jews believe…' and so on.
9. If children are withdrawn from RE, check the school policy and ensure that there is suitable alternative work for them to do in a suitable place. It may be set by the parents/carers.
10. Try to keep a balance between your own private feelings and the aspects of faith being taught. Compare in your mind how you might teach about the Romans or the Tudor period.
11. Approach RE in the same way as you would any subject: test the children's knowledge, understanding and evaluation

using assessment levels or End of Key Stage Statements and offer many opportunities to reflect and evaluate. Encourage children to contribute ideas, listen to each other, give their own viewpoints and ask questions.

12. Reflect on how to improve your RE lessons. Each year of teaching will add to your confidence.

13. Allow yourself time to prepare your lessons well, using DVDs, the creative arts and questioning techniques to encourage learning and reflection. The time is well spent!

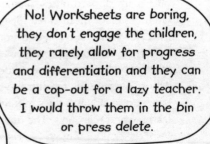

*

3. Planning RE

How does an RE teacher begin? The first place to look is in the locally agreed or appropriate syllabus.

Here is a process for teaching the Agreed Syllabus, which turns the long-term overview into a medium-term plan.

- Teacher's thinking time: The teacher identifies the area of RE to be studied in the long term from the appropriate syllabus.
- Teacher's thinking time: What are we trying to achieve? The teacher identifies the aims, learning objectives and learning outcomes using Attainment Targets 1 and 2. Use can be made of the 'I can...' statements on pages 66–68.
- Teacher plans how to organise the learning—how to connect the learning objective with the children's experience and with previous learning. (What do we already know? What do we want to know?) Activities are planned that match the learning objectives.
- Teacher plans active learning. This may include consideration of multiple intelligences, visual, auditory and kinesthetic learning. The child may be engaged in enquiring, enquiry-based learning and expression (see pages 25 and 93–94).
- Teacher plans for assessment. The assessment can be formative or summative (see page 63).
- Planning the plenary: How can the child show *what* has been learnt? How can the child show *how* he or she has learnt?

✳

4. RE learning cycle: a process for teaching and learning

There are many different learning cycles, and only one is offered here. A locally agreed syllabus might provide another model. It is important to ensure a structure to RE lessons that allows the four 'E's, **engage**, **enquire**, **express** and **evaluate**, to be part of the lesson.

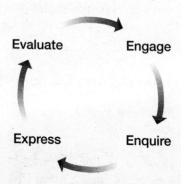

- **Engage:** The teacher engages the child by connecting the learning objective with the child's experience, or offers an experience within the classroom to 'hook' the children—for example, a story or a mystery bag with an artefact inside.
- **Enquire:** The child is helped to engage by the teacher's questioning, which invites them to think more deeply—for example, 'What questions would you want to ask Judas if he were here?' The children then offer questions that direct the learning enquiry—for example, 'Why is forgiveness so important to Christians?' They explore or research answers to their own lines of enquiry.

- **Express**: Children make their own responses individually or in groups to the story/questions/lesson content by offering their own interpretation using any aspect of their intelligence—for example, mathematical, creative or linguistic. They then reflect upon the meaning of the learning—for example, 'What does the parable of the mustard seed mean?'
- **Evaluate**: The children evaluate how they have learnt and what further questions they might want to ask, to direct the next area of learning. What would they like to learn about next in relation to the learning today?

The teacher will assess progress during the lesson, often intervening verbally, and may also assess summatively at the end of a unit against the learning outcomes.

A lesson example using the four 'E's model

This lesson example, for Key Stage 2, is based on the story of the ten lepers in Luke 17:11–19.

Learning objectives
- To discuss the importance for Christians of saying 'thank you'.
- To evaluate what the children think about saying 'thank you', compared with Christians.

Learning outcomes
- I can describe what a Christian might learn from the story of the ten lepers (Level 3).
- I can give reasons why the man returned to say 'thank you' (Level 4).
- I can evaluate why Christians think it is important to say 'thank you' and how that makes a difference to their lives (Level 5).
- I can compare what I think about saying 'thank you' with what Christians believe (Level 5).

Resources
- Pictures of six children and adults with leprosy.
- Three large sheets, preferably shaped as thought bubbles, one blank and the others with one of the following headings written on it: 'leper' or 'disciples'.
- Three pens.
- Ten sticky notes showing the letter 'L'.

Engage

In pairs, children discuss the following.

- How important do you think it is for you/Christians to say 'thank you'?
- Are there times when it is better not to say 'thank you'?
- How much do you care whether someone says 'thank you' to you or not?

Enquire

Tell the story of the ten lepers through teacher input and questioning to guide exploration and enquiry.

Teacher questions concerning the picture

Show the pictures of children and adults with leprosy and ask, 'What do you think these people have in common? What is leprosy?'

Teacher information

Leprosy is a disease in which a person's nerve endings are numb: they can't feel the ends of their fingers, for example. There is no feeling in them, so when the sufferers hurt themselves, there is no pain and their injuries can become infected. Many lepers have no fingers or toes. Leprosy is incurable. What might a leper find most difficult about life today?

Teacher narrative

This is a story about ten lepers. I need ten people to be lepers to help us to understand the story.

Ten volunteers are taken. A sticky note with a capital 'L' is placed on each of their foreheads to show they are lepers. They are asked to stand in one corner of the room, at the front, to show that they are just outside a village.

Addressing the lepers: You all have leprosy. No one wants to know you because you are infectious. You have had to leave your families in case they get the disease. You can't see your children or wife. No one will let you into their house. They keep clear of you when you walk down the street. What does that feel like? How do you feel?

The blank thought bubble is held first over one leper's head and then another's. As each leper makes a comment, their words are written on another large thought bubble under the heading 'Leper', by a teaching assistant or a child.

I need one volunteer to be Jesus and two to be disciples.

Jesus and the disciples stand at the front, away from the lepers.

Jesus was walking one day towards Jerusalem.

Ask Jesus and his friends to walk very slowly towards the lepers.

On their way, they met ten men who all had leprosy. As Jesus drew near to the lepers, they shouted out from a distance, 'Help us! Take pity on us!'

Hold the blank thought bubble over (a) the disciples' heads and (b) the lepers' heads.

What are you thinking?

The words are noted down by the teaching assistant or child on the appropriate headed thought bubble.

Jesus said to them: 'Go and show yourself to the priest and let him examine you.' When a leper was cured, he had to go to the priest. If the priest said he was well again, he would be allowed to go back to his family.

Hold blank thought bubble over one leper's head.

What are you thinking now? What are you feeling?

Words are recorded on the appropriate thought bubble by the teaching assistant or child.

The lepers turned around and started walking to the priest's house.

Ask the lepers to turn around and walk towards the priest's house.

On the way, the lepers looked at their hands and feet and saw that all their patches and sores had gone. They were better! The leprosy had gone.

Hold up the blank thought bubble again.

What are you feeling now?

The comments are recorded.

One leper, who was a foreigner, shouted out, 'Praise to God!', turned around and went straight back to Jesus. He fell down with his face to the ground and said, 'Thank you.'

Ask one leper to turn around and return to Jesus, looking delighted.

Jesus said, 'Where are the others? Has only one come to say "thank you"? Why is this foreigner the only one to come back? Get up and go, your faith has made you well.'

Hold the blank thought bubble over the disciples' heads.

What are you thinking?

The comments are recorded.

Express

Choose one of the people from the story and look at the words on the thought bubbles about the feelings generated. Choose one of the following activities.

- Make a design out of a few of the words, showing the story (a calligram).
- Select some of the words and reorder them to tell the story.
- Use some of the words to create a poem of any length.
- Create a rap, working in pairs.

The children may have other ideas, too. You must include the words 'thank you' in the work. If possible, also include the word 'faith'.

Evaluate and enquire further

In pairs, discuss the following questions.

- Why do you think the man said 'thank you'?
- Why did the others not return to say 'thank you'?
- What would you have done?
- Why do you think Jesus said, 'Your faith has made you well'?
- How important do you think it is, for Christians, to say 'thank you'? What difference does it make to them?
- How important do you think it is to say 'thank you'? Why?
- Are there any questions you would want to ask Jesus, the disciples or any of the lepers?
- Is there anything you would want to investigate further or learn about, having looked at this story from the New Testament?

Assessment

In pairs, the children decide which level they have reached.

What can I do?	No	Nearly	Yes
I can describe what a Christian might learn from the story of the ten lepers. (Level 3)			
I can give reasons why the man returned to say 'thank you'. (Level 4)			
I can evaluate why Christians think it is important to say 'thank you' and how that makes a difference to their lives. (Level 5)			
I can compare what I think about saying 'thank you' with what Christians believe. (Level 5)			

*

5. Enquiring and enquiry-based learning

The stages below are based upon a model offered in the arts and adapted by Ian Patience (see Appendix 4, page 93).

There are three images for the stages of enquiry: solid, liquid and gas.

- **Solid:** The learning is structured and teacher-directed. This image applies to a teacher offering structures and scaffolding learning. It includes activities in which the learners are able to make enquiries: for example, at the teacher's request, the children discuss the question 'Who was Jesus?' and use evidence provided by the teacher, including Bible texts, visual representations of Jesus and quotations from different faith communities. The children begin to be inducted into a culture of learning and enquiry in religious education.
- **Liquid:** The learning is negotiated and the teacher supports the child. The teacher helps the children to identify good ideas, questions or problems worth enquiring into and agrees their learning or enquiry focus with them. For instance, a group wants to explore the question 'What is a miracle?' or 'Who wrote the Bible?' The teacher provides support with resources and the process. Success indicators are negotiated and the way in which the group will evaluate the project is agreed. The teacher offers 'skilful neglect' to grant the children discovery space.
- **Gas:** The children devise their own line of enquiry or project. The teacher provides support and guidance when requested. There is flexible learning and assessment. The children may be given a day together to explore their enquiry.

*

6. Learning objectives in RE

The lesson example on pages 18–23 offers an outline. Although the exciting part of teaching is often the creative, planned activity for children, if the teacher does not think first about the RE learning objectives, the learning can be tenuous and not RE-focused. The learning objective when teaching any aspect from the Bible, for instance, needs to connect with the meaning or the purpose of the biblical writing.

If the learning objective for the parable of the lost sheep (Luke 15:1–7) is 'To know that a sheep was lost and found', the children may never understand that the story is about God. If the learning objective is 'To help children understand that Christians believe that God cares about everyone', there will be more opportunities for understanding the story.

However, the objective may disappear in an activity that involves making cotton wool sheep, with a lost sheep lying behind a bush on a large eye-catching display. The children may have had fun but they may not have learnt very much connected with the learning objective unless scaffolded questioning about what the story means has taken place.

The display can indicate the objective by connecting it with God. For example, a banner over the top, asking, 'How much do you think Christians believe that God cares for people?' with a question-and-answer sheet of sticky notes nearby, connects the 'woolly sheep' with the deeper meaning. 'I can' statements may help with ensuring that the right level of challenge has been set in the planning (see pages 66–68). Stronger RE lessons have both attainment targets within the learning objectives: sometimes Attainment Target 2 can implicitly also be about knowledge (Attainment Target 1).

❓ What if…?

What if I can't think of a learning objective that is 'theological' enough?

☺ Answer from a teacher

When I started teaching RE, I found it helpful to talk about the learning objectives with other teachers and ask them if they thought my learning objectives matched those of RE. It helped me to clarify what I was trying to do and made sure that I was teaching RE rather than only Literacy or another subject.

When teaching the parable of the lost son, I had asked the children to write a letter from the mother of the son to him after he had left home. Although this met a Literacy objective, it didn't meet any of the RE issues, concerning forgiveness or the concept of a loving God, that the parable includes. So, next time, after talking about relevant words and phrases, I asked them to write, draw or paint what someone might learn about God from the parable.

What makes a strong learning objective?

Here are some examples of weak and strong learning objectives for teaching Christianity. These can be used with staff training to open discussion on learning objectives in RE.

Learning objective	Comment
Noah (Old Testament) To know that the animals went into the ark in pairs.	**Weak** How does this help the child learn about what the story means? The story of Noah is about God's promise symbolised in the rainbow and the concept of 'new beginnings', with the family of Noah having the opportunity to start again.
Joseph (Old Testament) To know that Joseph had a multicoloured coat.	**Weak** Why does the teacher want the children to know that? The story of Joseph is about forgiveness and repentance. It is true that the musical *Joseph and the Amazing Technicolor Dreamcoat* shows Joseph with a many-coloured coat, but a more accurate translation is that he had a long-sleeved coat.
The Last Supper To know that Jesus and his disciples drank wine and ate bread at the Last Supper.	**Weak** Although this is basic knowledge (AT1), there can be more challenge in the learning objective—for example, 'Why is the Last Supper important to Christians?'

Baptism To understand why some Christians have a font in church and how it is used.	**Weak** This is factual knowledge only (AT1). The learning could become more challenging if the objective is to find out about a Christian's reasons for wanting baptism.
Prayer To know the words of the Lord's Prayer.	**Weak** This is factual knowledge only (AT1). It may be of importance, especially in church schools, but for RE to be more challenging, activities could include considering the meaning of each line. Why is the prayer important to Christians?
Hymns To be able to sing a Christian hymn.	**Weak** This is useful in a hymn practice in a church school, but not as an RE objective. It could become an RE objective if the meaning of the words of the hymn is explored and the children consider whether they think it represents Christianity well or not.
The crucifixion To know that Jesus died on a cross and compare his death with the death of Aslan in *The Lion, the Witch and the Wardrobe* by C.S. Lewis.	**Stronger** This is a beginning, but it would be better to include why the crucifixion is important to Christians.

The resurrection To show the feelings of the women who went to the tomb, through dance.	**Stronger** This is good in that it offers empathy and presumes knowledge of the account, although the teacher will need to be sensitive to the faith perspectives of children in the class and ensure that there is no personal compromise. More challenge could be offered by discussing the meaning of the resurrection for Christians.
Jesus To know that Jesus healed people out of compassion. To understand why Christians think the healing miracles are important. To understand how compassion motivates people.	**Strong** This is more challenging than simply expecting knowledge of a story. It relates to the children's own understanding of compassion.
Zacchaeus To understand why Zacchaeus was unpopular and consider what made him change his ways.	**Strong** This could work well. It includes both Attainment Targets 1 and 2.
Jesus stilling the storm To know the account of the stilling of the storm. To understand what it feels like to be still after being restless. To know that Christians believe Jesus can 'quieten' people.	**Strong** This could work well. It includes both Attainment Targets 1 and 2.

Once the learning objective has been decided, the teacher works out appropriate activities to ensure that high-quality learning is taking place, using the four 'E's. All planned activities must relate to the learning objective.

❓ What if…?

What if I planned a lesson for Year 2 with these learning objectives. Are they all right?

- To learn that Christians believe that God created the world in six days.
- To learn what was created on each day.

☺ Answer from a teacher:

I am not very happy with these learning objectives, for two reasons. (1) Some Christians believe that God created the world in six days and some do not. There is a chance for teachers to raise the question and lead a discussion here. (2) Why does it help children to know what happened on each day? I think it would be better for the children to understand how a creator loves their creation—for example, thinking about a painting or model they have made and their love for it.

One of the main points of the Genesis account is that there is only one creator God. Better learning objectives might be:

- To know that Christians believe that God made the world out of love.
- To know that Christians believe that there is only one God who created the world.

❓ What if…?

What if I planned a lesson for Year 3 on the parable of the sower and the seed, with these learning objectives?

- To know that seeds can't grow on hard ground.
- To be able to listen.

☺ Answer from a teacher

I think the parable is about how people notice or ignore the word of God, so better learning objectives might be:

- To consider how the seeds in the parable are like different sorts of people.
- To talk about why Jesus told this story.

Learning objectives, RE and the creative curriculum

The creative curriculum, which aims to promote a student's social, emotional and intellectual development, can lend itself to excellent RE. For instance, if Year 6 children are studying India, there is a richness of Hindu belief and culture to explore; or, if Year 2 are looking at different aspects of water, they might discover that many religions have water as an important symbolic part of their worship (for example, baptism in Christianity). It also offers opportunities for children to enquire in depth about religious issues.

In a school where the creative curriculum is taught, the RE subject leader needs to ensure that:

- the content of the agreed or appropriate syllabus is taught by the end of Key Stage 2.
- the RE learning objectives are mapped and clearly delivered within the curriculum.
- progression, as exemplified in the attainment targets, is clearly tracked across the Key Stages.

On some occasions, it may be necessary to teach RE discretely because it doesn't suit the chosen theme. The RE subject leader needs to be thoughtful and positive about where RE can fit in with the creative curriculum—and very clear about where it does not.

? What if...?

What if the whole school is looking at the story of *Charlie and the Chocolate Factory* by Roald Dahl? Where is the RE aspect?

☺ Answer from a teacher

Although the story is concerned with human relationships, greed, humility and poverty, and there are many opportunities for children to enhance their personal development through exploration of this exciting book, it is unlikely that there is part of your RE syllabus that you can connect here. You would be best teaching RE discretely for this theme and ensuring that the whole RE syllabus is covered.

✳

7. The RE policy document

An RE policy statement should be no longer than a side of A4 and should include:

- the religions that are taught at each Key Stage.
- the time allocated to RE.
- the frequency of themed days (if appropriate) during the year.
- assessment policy, which is usually the same as the whole-school policy, so it is a cross-reference.
- inclusion policy, which is usually the same as the whole-school policy, so it is a cross-reference.
- a statement on how many children are currently withdrawn from RE.

I like giving my opinion in RE.

8. Creating a variety of approaches to learning

There are many whole-school approaches to teaching and learning. Some schools use Kagan structures to engage children; other schools use the Teacher Effectiveness Programme (TEEP), Thinking Actively in a Social Context (TASC), Philosophy for Children (see an example on pages 55–57), accelerated learning and other approaches. Many involve training programmes, and more information is available on their websites.

All of these approaches can be useful in RE, and some RE subject leaders can be so enthused by one approach that, after they have introduced it in RE to the whole staff, it is rolled out to other curriculum areas.

Teaching the Bible

Teaching Bible stories can be daunting, but the process based on 'unpacking beliefs' in *Concept Cracking* by Trevor Cooling (see page 95) can offer hooks for teachers. The process is exemplified below, showing steps to teaching a Bible story, using Christmas as an example.

Step 1

First, unpack the beliefs, asking yourself, 'What are the beliefs embedded in the story? What are the possible meanings of the story?'

If you are unsure of the possible meanings, look up the story in a Bible commentary. In the Christmas story, the main belief is that God became human (the 'incarnation').

𝓕 Step 2

Decide which central meaning of the story you want to explore.

There is one major choice for this story—the incarnation—but another faith story, such as one of the parables, might have several meanings. Children engage well with working out possible meanings. The teacher does need to check that the belief is theological: for example, the story of Noah's ark is not a story about rescuing animals but about God's promise to the human race. The one meaning or belief chosen directs the lesson planning, but does not straitjacket the children's responses.

Write the learning outcomes to include Attainment Target 1 (learning about religion) and Attainment Target 2 (learning from religion). For example, learning outcomes for the Christmas story are:

- to be familiar with and engage creatively with the story of the birth of Jesus.
- to know that Christians believe that God became human in the form of Jesus.

𝓕 Step 3

Activity (a)

Ask yourself, 'How can I present this story to relate it to the children's experience?'

One of the best places to start is with the children's own experience, linking it into the lesson. For example, does any child have a baby brother or sister, or has anyone ever held a baby? Could you arrange for a baby to visit the classroom? The teacher gathers vocabulary to explain how a baby seems—for example, small, tiny, funny, vulnerable. The teacher may also gather vocabulary associated with a king and with God.

Enable the children to engage with the story using visualisation techniques, as follows.

Resources
- Small pieces of card and rough paper
- Felt-tip pens and pencils
- Pictures by Seurat or Monet, demonstrating pointillism

Explain that the children will hear a story they know well, but they will be asked to be part of the story. At the end they will be asked to create a picture.

Set up the room so that small pieces of card, pens, pencil and rough paper are available for each child at the end of the story.

Tell the story using the following script. The language can be adapted depending on the age of the children.

Sit as comfortably as you can, and, if it helps, close your eyes. I am going to tell you a story that you may have heard before and ask you to imagine that you are someone in the story. If you find it difficult, it doesn't matter—just sit quietly until I have finished.

Try to imagine that you are travelling back in time: 100 years... 200 years... right back to 2000 years ago. You are no longer in this room, and you are a grown-up man. You are tall, with a dark beard, and you live in a very hot country. You wear long robes to keep you cool, and the robe you are wearing today is pale brown. Your name is Joseph.

At the moment you are walking along a hot, dusty road by the side of the person you love most in the whole world. She is called Mary. She is sitting on a donkey to give her a rest because she is going to have a baby. She might have the baby any day: you look at her every so often as she is jolted along by the donkey. She never complains. You are both on your way to Bethlehem, because a law has just been passed that everyone must go back to the place where they were born, to be registered. You were born in Bethlehem and you wish now that you had been born somewhere else, because poor Mary looks very tired and pale. You long to help her more, but all you can do is to put your arm around her shoulders to support her when the donkey jolts. Your own feet begin to ache. The journey seems to be going on for ever.

At last, you see Bethlehem in the distance against the black, starry sky. There are all the buildings and tracks that you know so well from when you were a boy. By your side is Mary, who is looking more and more in pain. She smiles faintly when you announce that you have arrived, and you both make your way to the first hotel that you can find. To your horror, the man says that he has no room because everyone else has arrived that night to register, just like you. 'Never mind,' you hear yourself say to Mary. 'There are plenty of other places in Bethlehem.'

You both move slowly along to the next hotel, only to hear someone else being turned away as you arrive. Silently, you try the next one: that too is full. You feel like crying. You are so tired and you are very worried about Mary, who is clearly in pain and now has difficulty walking. You wonder why no one cares. Wearily, you try some more hotels, but they all give the same answer: 'We are full.' Then, just as you think you will have to sleep outside, one kind man looks sympathetically at Mary and says, 'Well, you can have the stable, if you like. I've just cleaned it out.'

You aren't sure. You would like better for Mary, but she seems only to want to lie down, and at least it will be private and sheltered. You accept gratefully and help Mary round to the stable, which is dark but warm inside. Very soon afterwards, the baby is born. You don't know much about babies, but a kind woman from the hotel helps. All you know for sure is that after the labour there is a beautiful baby boy.

You can't believe how tiny his hands and feet are and how perfectly formed. Mary is very calm now that the pain is over. She is glowing with happiness and very carefully wraps a cloth around the baby before laying him in the animals' food trough so that he can sleep.

You think that this is the most beautiful baby you have ever seen. You sit there in the glow of the single candle, wondering if anyone has ever been as happy as you. Suddenly, you hear a knock at the door. There in the entrance are some shepherds. You've never met them before. You have never even seen them. They ask if a baby has been born, and at first you are embarrassed, thinking that you may have all been too noisy, but you answer, 'Yes.' They tell you that while they were outside with the sheep on the hillside, they saw a bright light in the sky. It was so bright that it hurt their eyes, and an angel told them that the king, the Messiah, had at last been born in Bethlehem. So they hurried down to see the baby.

Then you remember. You remember that an angel had told you that this baby was going to be important to others. You look and look at the baby and at Mary in wonder.

I'd like you now gradually to leave Joseph in the stable as he wonders, and travel back through time through hundreds of years, back to today. You are no longer Joseph but yourself. You are sitting in your classroom, in this school, on this day. When you are ready, please look at me.

Then say to the class, 'Without speaking, on the rough paper draw any shape that you heard in the story. It might be a triangle or an oval. You can draw any number of shapes. Now write the names of any colours that you saw.'

Show some examples on the whiteboard of French artists who painted using dots to create a scene (for example, Seurat) and explain that this artistic movement is called 'pointillism' because of the small dots used to make the picture.

The children use the felt-tip pens on the small pieces of card to create their own picture from the story, in the style of pointillism.

Display every card immediately on the wall.

Activity (b)

Ask yourself, 'What activity will help the children to understand the meaning of the story and also match the learning objectives?'

The children have become familiar with and have empathised with the Christmas story. They now need to wrestle with the understanding that Christians believe that Jesus is God in human form. Assuming that some prior learning has been carried out on the roles and characteristics of God as seen in the Old Testament (for example, king, judge, powerful, loving), they now complete a 'Think Pair share' activity. Ask: 'If you were any god as seen in the Roman myths or any other story, and you wanted people to know you loved them, how would you show yourself today? Why?' Be aware of sensitivities to this activity for some children.

In groups, pupils choose one way in which God might show love to people, then create a collage on A3 paper. The pictures are placed around a class nativity set, which has the title 'Christians believe God became a human to show God's love'.

Step 4

Ask yourself, 'What is the main theological idea and how is it relevant to the children?'

Draw out the meaning and interpretations of the story from the children. Children write their answers on Christmas cards to the questions 'What do you think it means to Christians that God became a baby? What do you think Christians say God is like?' The cards are placed in front of the nativity set.

As an assessment task, in pairs, one child tells another as much as they know of the story of the birth of Jesus. The other child explains what it shows about Christians' belief in God. They both say if they agree with that view or not, and why.

❓ What if…?

What if a child takes part in a guided visualisation and tells their parents that they have been 'meditating'? The parents think that the children have been opening their minds to 'nothingness' and complain.

☺ Answer from a teacher

You would need to talk to the parent and show the lesson plan and the script. Explain that what you are doing is helping children to enter a story imaginatively. You are making sure that they know when the visualisation begins and when it ends, and that, although they are being asked to imagine they are Joseph, they know at the end who they really are.

Also, most importantly, you are not asking the children any open-ended questions such as 'You reach an open door—what do you see through it?' Such questions can cause deep psychological harm because they can open up past distress, and teachers are not trained to deal with such possible traumas. For that reason, I would only use guided visualisations with stories.

Other possible strategies for meeting the learning objective in RE (or any lesson)

Strategy	Example
Artefacts	Use a mystery bag containing a *yad* as an introduction to the importance of Jewish Torah. Ask questions about a *murti* (image) of Shiva.
Reflective storytelling (see page 95: *More Bible Storybags*)	Use simple knitted figures to help the children actively engage with the meaning behind Bible stories. The story of Adam and Eve in *More Bible Storybags* focuses upon the breaking of friendship with God, the concept of 'peace', and artistic expressions of the story.
Card sorting	Sort the ten commandments into positive and negative commands, or use diamond sorting to rank their importance or how hard they are to follow.
Continuum	Choose one end of the room for 'strongly agree' and the other for 'strongly disagree'. Children place themselves on a line between the two ends, according to their opinion on questions such as 'I think Christians should never go to war' or 'I think babies shouldn't be baptised, so that they can decide when they are older what they believe.'
Conscience alley	Two rows of children create a gangway for one child to walk down. One row calls out negatively concerning a decision and the other positively. The child decides what she will then do. For example, to the shepherd deciding whether to return and find a single lost sheep, one row calls out 'Don't go back—your other sheep need you' and the other tries to persuade him that he should look for the sheep.

Choral narration	The story (of any faith) is told through choral chanting. In groups, the children make up words to describe any one aspect of a story—for example, using words ending in 'ing'. Each group practises its choral contribution and the groups are then put together to tell the whole story.
Freeze frame	Children choose three parts of a story (for example, David and Goliath) and work out a freeze frame for each part, for others to guess.
Hot seat	The teacher or a child takes on the role of a person (for example, Moses). The class submits questions in advance about who they are and what they did. This has to be carefully managed to ensure engagement.
ICT	Children research and design their own PowerPoint presentations—for example, to tell why Christians think forgiveness is important.
Items to include in a story	A few items (such as two coins, a staff, a book, a shawl and a picture of a pair of eyes) are given to a group of children, who are asked to use them to act out the story of the widow's mite (Mark 12:41–44).
Making art	Children create a picture in the style of an artist (for example, Lowry) to show the most important part of Holy Week.
Mantle of the expert	Any one child becomes an expert (for example, on Judaism) and is asked questions.
Mime to revise	One child mimes something that he or she has learnt in RE and the class guesses what it is.
Music	Children create a song or rap to tell the story of the escape from Egypt in the book of Exodus.

Newspaper reports/ interviews/diary entries/DVD	Children write a newspaper report on Jesus stilling the storm, or imagine an interview with Martin Luther King, or imagine being an eyewitness to Jesus washing the disciples' feet.
Overheard conversations	Ask, 'What do you think the disciples would have said to each other after seeing the feeding of the five thousand?'
Poetry	Use a poetic form, such as haiku (a three-line poem of five syllables followed by seven syllables then five syllables), to write about the healing of the blind man.
Role play	Children are given the role of a character in the story and improvise in front of the class. This can be repeated to allow all who want to act to have a chance.
Questions box/wall	Children write any questions that puzzle them, from the lesson or more generally, and place them in a brightly decorated box or on the wall. The teacher takes time in each lesson to ask others how they would answer the question.
Sharing group work	Pairs decide on questions they want to ask a Sikh visitor to the classroom. Each pair shares their questions with another pair and they agree together on the best two questions to ask.
Slow motion	The children act an event (for example, Diwali) in slow motion.
Text or email	Children imagine that they are witnesses to the healing of Jairus' daughter or the resurrection or Paul's conversion, and send a text with a photograph on their mobile phone to a friend. What would they say? What picture would they take?

Using a picture	Before teaching the parable, show Rembrandt's picture *The Prodigal Son* (downloadable from the internet). Ask the children, 'What can you see? What's happening? What question would you ask the artist?' Compare the picture with other, more recent, paintings of the prodigal son.
Who am I?	Looking back over a few lessons, the teacher and children take it in turns to choose a character (such as Abraham, a rabbi, a Muslim child or the Buddha). As a class or in groups of four, the children have to guess who it is in no more than ten questions.

*

9. Visits and visitors

There is nothing better than a visit to a place of worship to enhance and embed learning about religion. Staff can also find it invaluable for their own professional development.

Before the visit

- Visit the place, talk with the faith leaders and find out any customs that are expected—for example, taking shoes off, covering heads.
- Confirm that the children will bring questions with them and be clear about what you hope the children will learn. The place of worship may request a contribution rather than a charge per child.
- Prepare the children by telling them what to expect. As with any visit, prepare an activity booklet to engage their learning.

After the visit

- As with any visit, send a 'thank you' letter from the class.
- If the subject leader, for any reason, cannot take the children to a place of worship, use can be made of guided tours on the internet and photographs. A classroom can be adjusted to show the layout of, for example, a church or mandir.
- If a visitor is invited into the classroom, it is advisable for the children to prepare questions beforehand.

*

10. Using religious artefacts

Religious artefacts bring children into contact with the actual objects used by believers in the course of practising their faith. Consequently, they should be handled (and stored) reverently. Artefacts allow hands-on experience and have the potential to arouse curiosity so that children engage in questioning. They should be used in conjunction with visits, visitors and photographs to bring religions to life.

Do

- Find out as much as possible about the artefact first.
- Make links with children's experiences.
- Make links with other aspects of human/religious experience.
- Make links (where possible) with other aspects of the curriculum.
- Encourage children to question: see how many questions children can think of about the artefact.
- Treat artefacts with respect.
- Encourage pupils to be sensitive with what other people consider sacred.

Don't

- Store or handle artefacts in a disrespectful way.
- Mix objects together as if they are from the same religion.
- Assume that 'lots is good'. A simple artefact such as a lapel badge can stimulate much rich discussion.

Examples of religious artefacts with suggested activities

Artefacts: palm cross (representing a palm leaf), chalice, piece of rough wood, long nail, stone for empty tomb, myrrh

Activity: One of each of the artefacts above is given to a small group of children. The children decide what part it played in the story of Holy Week and Easter Day. They write a short piece together, beginning, 'I am a...' For example, they might write, 'I am a palm leaf. I heard shouts around me and suddenly felt myself being pulled off the tree...' If possible, they should finish by describing the way they felt.

When they are ready, one member of each group holds the artefact and another reads out what has been written. The groups follow on sequentially so that the story is told through to Easter. This activity can be used to embed the learning or to revise it.

Artefact: icon

An icon is a 'window to God'. Painting an icon is an act of worship and is carried out prayerfully. Icons portray Jesus or the saints, depicted with their full face always showing and without any shadows. When completed, the icon is used in worship in the home or church. Worshippers pray before icons and kiss them to show their respect. The teacher can download images from the internet, but one actual icon is helpful for children to see.

Activity: Look at the icon. What can you see? How does it make you feel? What questions can you ask?

Describe the icon to your partner. What do you notice about the colours or expressions?

What does the phrase 'An icon is a window to God' mean?

Do you think Christians could worship the picture rather than God?

Artefact: prayer beads

Muslims may pray using a string of 33 or 99 beads, called *subha* (or *misbahah*). The beads are threaded loosely on a string with a knotted end, and finished off with a tassel. The beads are passed through the fingers as Muslims say a prayer such as 'God is great' or reflect on the 99 beautiful names of Allah.

Activity: How many names of God can you think of? What do the names tell us about Allah? How do you think having prayer beads helps Muslims to pray?

After looking at the 99 names of Allah, children could make a set of clay beads, grouping the beads into 33s and using symmetrical patterns on the beads. Which name of Allah appeals to you most?

Artefact: representation of Buddha

There are many different representations of Buddha, reflecting the Mahayana and Theravada strands of Buddhism. There are depictions of Buddha touching earth, in a gesture of compassion and giving, meditation, reassurance and teaching.

Activity: What do you like about this depiction of the Buddha and how does it make you feel?

What do you think the positions of his hands mean?

What kind of material has been used to make the Buddha? What effect does this have?

What question would you want to ask about the Buddha?

Artefact: prayer mat

Muslims are required to perform ritual prayer (*salah*) five times a day. On each occasion they must lie down before God, kneeling on the ground with their foreheads touching it. Each prayer mat should have an arch design on it, so that it is laid down in the correct direction for prayer, pointing towards Makkah. The prayer mats may show the Kaaba and the Prophet Muhammad's mosque in Madinah. Occasionally there is a compass sewn into the prayer mat.

Activity: What colours and patterns can you see in the prayer mat?

Using symmetrical designs, the children can design and weave a prayer mat. There must be no images of animals or people included.

How would the prayer positions help a Muslim to pray? What is the significance of posture in prayer?

Why do you think a 'personal' prayer mat might be important?

Artefact: prayer shawl

The *tallit* is a prayer shawl worn by Jewish males. It is wrapped around the shoulders or over the head during prayer. There are 613 fringes because there are that many commandments (*mitzvoth*) in the Torah.

Activity: How do you think a boy would feel wearing the *tallit* for the first time?

Why do you think believers have special clothes for worship? How would it help them?

How much is prayer an 'inner' or an 'outer' activity?

How do I deal with big questions? A child asked me why her brother was in a wheelchair and no one else was. What should I have said?

Always take big questions seriously and say when you really don't know the answer. The reply will depend upon discerning exactly what the child is asking, and on whether or not you know her brother. One possible reply might be: 'We don't know why some people have illnesses and disabilities, but we do know that your brother makes life happy for everyone around him.'

11. Responding to difficult questions

RE is one of the areas of the curriculum where children are sparked to ask questions about life and death, suffering and evil. If they are asking the questions, the teacher knows that the lesson has given them the opportunity and should be gratified that there is an atmosphere of safety and enquiry within the classroom which makes the child comfortable enough to ask questions. All questions need to be taken seriously to affirm and value the child's wish to enquire and explore.

> **❓ What if…?**
> What if I get asked a difficult question such as, 'What happens when you die?'
>
> **☺ Answer from a teacher**
> I always find it helpful to think about how I would answer a difficult question in Maths or History that I didn't know enough about. On those occasions I would say, 'That's a great question, let's find out' or 'What does anyone else think?' I might ask the child to answer their own question: 'What do *you* think?' I try hard never to show that it is too difficult to answer, since all questions are worthy of exploration and discussion. At its best, it can lead to new learning and a new RE project.

The skilled teacher begins to discern whether the question is one that will take the lesson in a different direction for everyone or just for that child. It is always acceptable for a teacher to say, 'I don't know' to a child's question, indicating that even many adults don't know the answer.

The teacher needs first to be absolutely certain that they have understood the child's question.

A story: What is the child really asking?

The teacher roamed around the room, looking at the children's group work. They were making models of a present-day nativity scene in a bus shelter or under a bridge. Suddenly a Year 3 child put her hand up. The teacher walked over and the girl said, 'How did Mary know she was going to have a baby?' The teacher paused, considering where to start and how much information to give. As she paused, the girl's friend said, 'The angel Gabriel told her.' 'Oh yes, of course,' said the girl, and carried on with what she was doing.

❓ What if…?

What if a child tells me he doesn't believe in God? I am a Christian and very keen that everyone should know about how God loves them.

☺ Answer from a teacher

I always try to remember that RE is not about me or my beliefs, but about raising the questions to help the pupils think critically, enquire, reflect and evaluate. I would ask the child to give their reasons and ask others in the class to give reasons for the opposite view. The pupils could then have a valuable discussion about belief and learn that others may differ from themselves.

❓ What if…?

What if a child asks, 'How do Christians take Holy Communion?' There are so many different ways to answer.

☺ Answer from a teacher

I always find it helpful to use the phrase 'Some Christians…' or 'Some Jews…' and so on. The diversity is so great within faith communities that a teacher can rarely say 'All Christians…' There are even different understandings about the resurrection. Children seem to respect the diversity within religions and I have found that this approach avoids stereotyping, too.

Encouraging questions

One aspect of spiritual development is curiosity. In RE, teachers can encourage curiosity by helping children to ask their own questions. One approach that helps to raise and explore questions is 'Philosophy for Children' (P4C). This allows children to discuss open-ended 'big questions'.

RE can use the P4C approach to introduce stories of faith from which children will naturally begin to ask and suggest answers to 'big questions'. Matthew Lipman, who introduced the process, said that there are three major concerns of philosophy:

- To think as clearly and logically as possible.
- To show the relevance of such thinking to the problems that one confronts.
- To think in ways that search out fresh alternatives and open up new options.

Such concerns are also the aims of quality RE.

How can P4C be introduced into RE? Below is a suggested way of introducing the story of Jonah.

> **Resources**
> - A DVD of the story of Jonah or an artistic representation or picture of a very large fish to act as a stimulus

The teacher connects the work on Yom Kippur with the story of Jonah being read in the synagogue.

Ask: 'Have you ever wanted to hide or run away from something? Why? What happened?'

This story is about someone who tried to run away from God. Explain that we will see the story and then talk about what is puzzling or unusual in the story.

- **Stimulus:** The story of Jonah is shown on a DVD (in a short version) and followed by role play to help the children to remember the story.
- **Response:** On their own, children write down their answers to: 'What question would you want to ask about the story?'
- **Paired question creation:** The children tell their partner their question. They agree on one question to ask about the story. In

groups of four, children agree on the most interesting question.

- **Elect focus for the enquiry:** The teacher leads a class vote for the question to discuss. The pair who asked the question say why they asked it, to introduce the discussion.
- **Assumptions in/interpretation of question:** The teacher leads a discussion on the question—for example, 'What do you think about the question? What does it mean? Do you agree with…? Why?'
- **Enquire and express:** 'What do you think the answer is? What are the possibilities? What are the different solutions?' The teacher/facilitator may use questions such as 'What reasons do you have for saying that? Why do you agree (or disagree) on that point? How are you defining the word you have just used? What do you mean by that? What follows from what you just said?'
- **Stop halfway to reflect on progress:** 'How far have we got? We have agreed that…' The teacher puts the comments up on the flipchart.
- **Enquiry towards conclusion:** The teacher indicates that time is running out. How can we draw the discussion to a conclusion?
- **Reflection on progress:** The teacher invites everyone to make a statement about their response: 'Have you anything to say about what we have just done?'
- **Evaluate and review:** Comments are invited on the process: 'Where could we go next with this discussion? What have you learnt today? Do you know how you learnt it?'

For more information about Philosophy for Children and details of training, visit www.sapere.org.uk.

12. What mistakes might I make?

There are plenty of mistakes to be made in RE! Most important for a teacher is a willingness to take risks, to try out new ways of teaching and to learn from mistakes. A teacher needs an open mind and a desire to learn from others, especially from the children. One teacher said that Hindus believe in many gods. He realised his error after overhearing a Hindu girl saying that she could never be a Christian because Christians worship three gods (Father, Son and Holy Spirit), whereas Hindus worship one god, Brahman. He corrected his mistake by raising the question with the whole class.

❓ What if...?
What if I offend the local Muslim community in my teaching?

☺ Answer from a teacher
If you have any doubts, ask the Muslim children and their parents before you teach any new concept. Remember that all faiths include diversity and it is important to represent that diversity as much as possible.

I love it when we do drama in RE. It helps me remember what we learnt.

Drama and role play can be very useful tools to engage children and embed learning. Some of the challenges they present are listed below in the form of Dos and Don'ts.

Do	Don't
Use drama and role play wherever possible to engage children in meeting the learning objective.	Represent the Jewish concept of God, Allah, Muhammad or a Sikh guru in any human form, even with hot-seating.
Make pupils aware when they are acting and taking part in a role play by marking the start and finish—for example, with a Buddhist singing bowl or a bell.	Use the 'actual' sacred texts as props in the drama or role play, since it may cause offence.
Use stories in role play from all traditions, but be aware of sensitive areas. For example, when using religious artefacts, some Christians may be comfortable with dressing up in priests' robes, while others may not. In Judaism, if a child who is not a Jew wears a *kippah*, rather than being helpful, it can become 'silly'. The lesson can then encourage prejudice rather than nurture understanding.	Use religious artefacts in role play as objects of worship.
Consult with local faith leaders, where possible, if you are unsure about any activity.	Role play worship, since there is a fine line between the role play and the worship, which may be misconstrued.
Remember that all faith communities have a variety of interpretations of their faith.	

❓ What if...?

What if a parent helped a Year 4 class to create a display of calligraphy showing the name of Allah and words from the Qur'an in bright colours, and then a Muslim parent complained because the name of Allah was placed at the bottom of the display?

☺ Answer from a teacher

It is important to remember always to place the name of Allah as high as possible in any display. Also, always place the Qur'an on the highest shelf available in a room. Muslims create complex symmetrical patterns rather than pictures of animals or people, to show that there is no idolatry and nothing is worshipped except Allah.

I have always found it helpful to consult with parents or local people of faith about what they recommend and why. However, in some schools, the diversity within faiths means that there is often a variety of practices, so you may receive different answers. These answers in themselves can be useful for classroom discussion.

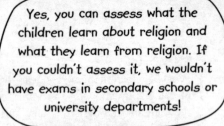

*

13. Assessing RE

Children are assessed **summatively** and **formatively**. The two are often intertwined and are sometimes indistinguishable. The assessment activity is an integral part of teacher planning.

Assessment of learning (summative assessment)

Assessment of Learning (AoL) offers a snapshot summary of where children are at any one time. This can be a half-termly assessment on a given task against the assessment levels. Children can then set their own targets for the next half-term.

Assessment for learning (formative assessment)

'Assessment for Learning is the process of seeking and interpreting evidence for use by learners and their teachers to decide where the learners are in their learning, where they need to go and how best to get there' (Assessment Reform Group, 2002).

Assessment for Learning (AfL) informs the next steps to learning. The teacher might feed back in writing to say how a child could improve next time, or the teacher can ask a class to 'traffic light' their understanding; if a few children hold up red, the teacher realises that the lesson needs to revisit some of the learning.

❓ **What if…?**
What if a teacher tells me they can't assess RE because the children always have very good discussions in her lessons and there is no time to write anything down?

🙂 **Answer from a teacher**

I wonder what her learning objectives are for the lessons: I expect she can assess against those. She might provide sticky notes for children to write their views on the lesson—for example, answering the question 'What did I learn?' She might look at one or two children in each lesson and review progress as they talk to each other. I wonder if she offers a variety of ways of engaging with religion in her lessons.

The RE subject leader can support colleagues by having samples of assessed work in RE, with explanations of how the work meets the level. The samples should contain a variety of creative ways of learning in RE and may include recorded responses, collaborative work, art, music or drama. A few lesson plans can show how peer assessment is included in RE.

A subject leader can be well informed about children's progress by looking at the assessment of a small mixed sample of children for each year group and gathering samples of their work. The children can be interviewed to check for understanding and the way they like to learn best in RE.

> RE is about thinking hard, as you have to really think about other people's thoughts and then help them to think even more about it—and that's not easy.

Assessment levels

The levels of assessment are a guide for teachers as they plan a series or one lesson. Many teachers find the pupil-speak 'I can...' statements easier to use than the levels from the non-statutory national framework for RE (2004). The two attainment targets commonly used are Learning about religion (Attainment Target 1) and Learning from religion (Attainment Target 2).

- Learning about religion (AT1)
  - ❖ Beliefs and teachings (what people believe)
  - ❖ Practices and lifestyles (what people do)
  - ❖ Expression and language (how people express themselves)

- Learning from religion (AT2)
  - ❖ Identity and experience (making sense of who we are)
  - ❖ Meaning and purpose (making sense of life)
  - ❖ Values and commitments (making sense of right and wrong)

Although assessment levels are not used in all other subject areas, the RE teacher may still find them helpful to measure progression in RE. Some Agreed Syllabi offer End of Key Stage statements in RE. The RE teacher should aim for:

- assessment tasks or assessments for learning that clearly match the learning objectives.
- a summative assessment once a term.
- formative assessment included within the lessons.

Assessment is not confined to the written task, but can be creative. It can focus on, for instance, role play within one group for one week and then a different group another week, so that during the course of the term each child has been assessed for their role play in RE. Best practice incorporates AT1 and AT2 into every lesson.

'I can…' statements are mapped to levels in the chart below:

Level 1

AT1
- I can remember a Christian (or other faith) story and talk about it.
- I can recognise objects that are special to Christians (or Hindus and so on).
- I can recognise religious symbols and words and talk about them.

AT2
- I can talk about things that happen to me.
- I can talk about what I like or dislike in a story.
- I can talk about what is important to me and why.

Level 2

AT1
- I can say some things that people believe about God and tell a Christian (or other faith) story.
- I can talk about some of the things that are the same for different religious people.
- I know what some Christian (or other faith) symbols stand for and I can say what some of the art (or music and so on) is about.
- I can talk about what is important to others and to those who have a religious belief, with respect for their feelings.

AT2
- I can talk about what happens to others, with respect for their feelings.
- I can talk about some things in stories that make people ask questions.
- I can talk about some things that are wrong and some things that are right.

Level 3

AT1

- I can describe what a believer might learn from a religious story.
- I can describe how and why believers use holy books (or places, stories and so on).
- I can identify the religious beliefs that may be contained in religious art (or music and so on).

AT2

- I can compare some of the things that influence me with those that influence other people.
- I can compare my ideas about life with those of other people.
- I can link the things that are important to me and other people to the way I behave and think.
- I can ask important questions about religion.

Level 4

AT1

- I can make comparisons between the beliefs and ideas of some religions and show how they are connected to believers' lives.
- I can express beliefs/ideas/feelings in styles and words used by believers and explain what they mean.
- I can describe how people show that religion is important in their lives.

AT2

- I can ask questions about what influences the lives of believers and suggest appropriate answers.
- I can explain different things that might be involved in belonging to a religion.
- I can ask questions about life and suggest appropriate answers, with reference to some religions.
- I can ask questions about the decisions people make (including believers) and I can suggest what might happen as a result of different decisions.

Level 5

AT1

- I can recognise some of the main beliefs/ideas shared by some religions and can explain how these make a difference to the lives of believers.
- I can recognise some of the main practices shared by some religions and can explain how these make a difference to the lives of believers.
- I can compare similarities and differences within and between religions.
- I can use what I have learned in RE to compare my views about moral issues with those of others, including believers.
- I can explain how some religions provide answers to ultimate questions.

AT2

- I can use what I have learned in RE to compare my identity and my experience with that of others, including believers.
- I can use what I have learned in RE to compare my ideas about life with those of others, including believers.
- I can explain some of the challenges that belonging to a religion involves.

Level 6

AT1

- I can show my understanding of religious beliefs, practices and ideas and how they may belong to a particular group within a religion. I can see reasons for people's beliefs and ideas, whether or not I agree with them.
- I can show my understanding of how religious beliefs and ideas may be expressed in different ways and how groups or individuals may use particular forms of expression.
- I can use religious and philosophical vocabulary to talk about religion and beliefs.

AT2

- I can relate different religious perspectives on the meaning of life to my own and others' views.
- I can relate different religious perspectives on a range of contemporary values to my own and others' views.
- I can explain some of the challenges about values and commitment that belonging to a religion involves.

❓ What if...?

What if I had a colleague who taught a lesson on Moses and the burning bush to Year 5 with the learning objective 'For pupils to be able to retell the story of Moses and the burning bush'. He gave an assessment task of 'Draw a cartoon of what happened when Moses met the burning bush.' This meant that the level the pupils were aiming to reach was: 'I can remember a Christian story' (Level 1). What should I do as subject leader?

☺ Answer from an RE subject leader

This lesson was clearly too low a level of challenge for the age of the class. You could lead staff INSET on the assessment levels and discuss how to challenge pupils. If the teacher is asking for your advice, you could make suggestions to show how he could have challenged the pupils further and raised expectations—for example, hot-seating Moses to find out why he took any notice of the voice, and interviewing a Christian visitor to the class to ask what the story means to them and how it makes a difference to their lives. To challenge the more able pupils further, they could answer the question 'How is Moses' experience of meeting God similar to or different from Paul's experience on the road to Damascus?' The comparison can be made with any biblical figure or with a contemporary believer. The pupils can then be assessed using the 'I can' statements as below.

- I can describe what a Christian might learn from the story of Moses and the burning bush.
- I can ask questions about the decisions Moses made as a result of seeing the burning bush.
- I can explain similarities and differences within religions.

Important note

One of the aims of religious education is to reduce prejudice and discrimination and enhance understanding of religion. If the RE teacher is not careful, there can be the opposite effect. If a teacher emphasises or only teaches Attainment Target 1, 'Learning about religion', the children can become prejudiced. They can gain knowledge without understanding and use that knowledge against other faith groups. By learning only about the practices of Christianity or Sikhism, for example, children can gain ammunition to hurt others. If the lesson includes empathy, the child's own experiences and engagement (Attainment Target 2), it is more likely that the children will want to engage and dialogue with other faiths rather than feeling threatened. When the creative arts are used well to teach world religions, prejudice and discrimination are likely to be reduced.

*

14. What do I need to do as a subject leader in RE?

The role of the subject leader is as follows.

1. To know
Know about the subject:
- The Agreed Syllabus/diocesan or relevant syllabus and the Schemes of Work
- Any big issues in RE
- How RE can contribute to spiritual, moral, social and cultural development
- Theories of learning to support RE

Know about practice in RE in the school:
- What happens in all the RE across the school

Know about resources:
- What resources there are in school
- What further resources are needed
- What's available electronically at no cost
- How the resources are deployed across the school

Know about attainment:
- Attainment levels in school and, if appropriate, end of Key Stage statements
- Comparisons with local and national attainment

2. To support
Support colleagues with planning, by:
- Writing an RE policy
- Drawing up an RE content outline
- Assisting with short-term planning

Support colleagues with teaching, by:
- Demonstrating good practice
- Working alongside colleagues
- Providing advice

Support governors, non-teaching staff, parents and children:
- With information and opportunities for involvement

3. To monitor

Monitor attainment by:
- Identifying trends
- Making comparisons
- Knowing about different groups (for example, boys, girls, SEN, more able and so on) in RE
- Setting and reviewing targets

Monitor plans by:
- Comparing plans with expectations
- Checking for clarity of intended outcomes
- Checking for differentiation

Monitor teaching by:
- Observing and providing feedback

Monitor children's work by:
- Sampling

4. To change and develop RE
- By building on existing good practice
- By overcoming any weaknesses
- By striving for continuous improvement
- By networking with local schools, both primary and secondary
- By leading professional development on RE in local RE hubs
- By considering how RE can make global links
- By considering how the children can help direct the learning in RE

❓ What if…?

What if I am a teaching assistant and am asked to be responsible for RE?

☺ Answer from an RE subject leader

This is a real compliment and to be taken seriously. If you feel passionate about the subject and you have a good line manager, then accept it. Remember:

- Request ongoing professional development to ensure that you understand current thinking. There are long-distance learning courses you can take.
- Find other RE teachers and ask them about RE in their schools.
- It is not a Sunday school but a school, and RE is an educational subject on a par with any other subject.
- Always ask questions if in any doubt.
- Keep your enthusiasm!

What about self-evaluation?

In order to improve religious education in a school, the subject leader will need to reflect upon and review the subject. The subject leader takes whole-school priorities as part of the action plan and includes others from their own self-evaluation. The self-evaluation form below is an example to help the subject leader. It is best completed with colleagues ticking the first or second column and then agreeing the action points together. The RE Quality Mark website evidence form offers a more comprehensive list for self-evaluation for subject leaders (see www.reqm.org/awards). The third column will inform the RE action plan for the coming year, which can then be given to the governing body.

	Not achieved	Achieved	Planned action
Learning			
Children in each Key Stage make good progress in RE			
Children have opportunities every term to learn in RE through: • art • music • poetry • drama • ICT			

Assessment takes place: • summatively, using assessment levels • formatively for every child during lessons			
Teachers use high-order questioning skills in RE			
Children are enthusiastic about their learning in RE			
RE planning			
RE follows the locally agreed or appropriate syllabus			
Religious concepts underpin the RE planning and learning			
RE curriculum plans for opportunities for spiritual, moral, social and cultural development			

What do I need to do as a subject leader in RE?

RE lessons plan equal opportunities for 'learning about' religion and 'learning from' religion			
Visits are planned for each Key Stage in RE			
The classroom has visitors in RE at each Key Stage			
Subject leadership			
There is a clear vision for RE in the school			
The governors are informed about RE regularly and offer challenge and support			
RE priorities are informed by whole-school priorities			
RE policies connected with whole-school policies are in place: • assessment policy • SMSC policy			

Monitoring processes for RE are in place and inform future planning			
Parents are well informed about RE and supportive			
RE is resourced with: • artefacts • DVDs • recent and stimulating pictures • art materials • music • digital camera • computer • lists of appropriate website links for particular lessons			
Classrooms and school areas have stimulating RE displays that challenge children to think			

Continuing Professional Development			
All staff have opportunities for RE CPD			
All RE CPD has a clear impact upon children			

The RE subject leader may find the evidence form for the RE Quality Mark a helpful document for self-evaluation. It is freely downloadable from www.reqm.org.

I like the way RE helps us to show respect for others.

What should there be in an RE handbook?

The subject leader needs to have a file to show their knowledge of RE in their school. The school will have its own policy on subject handbooks. There is no need for the collation of a handbook to be burdensome, nor should it include too much content.

The following checklist shows what should be included.

Section 1

- Vision statement and subject aims
- Religious Education Policy
- How RE links with Spiritual, Moral, Social and Cultural development (SMSC)
- Time allocation for RE at each Key Stage
- Deployment of staff (if relevant)

Section 2

- Overview of the long-term planning referenced to the appropriate syllabus—for example, when each religion is studied
- Visits/visitors that support subject work

Section 3

- Assessment policy
- Data indicating progress in RE (including special needs children and more able children)

Section 4

- Subject development plan for current year
- Previous subject development plans with evaluations that feed forward into the current plan

Section 5

- Monitoring schedule for the year
- Any reports/feedback as a result of monitoring
- Details of evaluation and action taken
- Relevant staff meeting minutes, and so on

Section 6

- Details of training planned
- Details of training undertaken in/out of school by subject leader and/or other staff
- Impact of the CPD upon RE

Another folder should have:

- **Planning:** Medium and short-term planning for RE
- **Resources:** List of resources
- **Assessment:** Teacher assessments and annotated samples of work

What are some of the challenges for a subject leader?

❓ What if…?

What if I have a Jehovah's Witness parent who wants her child to be withdrawn from RE, but the child loves RE? What should I do?

☺ Answer from a teacher

It is the parents' legal right to withdraw their child, and they do not need to give a reason. I have found that it always helps to meet the parents with the head teacher first and explain the syllabus and activities you teach, plus the visits that you make. You can then explain that you are not indoctrinating but helping children to understand about other people's beliefs. In the past I have invited the parents to join the class in a lesson. If, however, they still wish to withdraw, then that is their right and you must graciously accept it. Don't take it personally; you have done everything you can!

❓ What if…?

What if a parent won't let a child go on a visit to a mosque for religious reasons?

☺ Answer from a teacher

When this happened to me, I asked the head teacher to explain to the parents that it was part of the learning and not about 'conversion'. The parents weren't very happy, so I invited them on a visit that I had planned, with the staff. They became enthusiastic and then allowed their child to attend. In the end, it is the parents' right, but it's a pity if a child has to miss out on such a valuable learning experience.

❓ What if...?

What if I love RE, but the staff say they haven't got time to do it and are not inspired? What can I do?

☺ Answer from a teacher

Firstly, keep smiling! Secondly, don't lose your enthusiasm. You could take the staff to a local place of worship on an INSET day, or invite a visitor to talk about their faith. You could take good resources in to school and talk about how to use them at a meeting.

✳

— Appendices —

*

— Appendix 1 —

What does the law say about RE?

The Education Act (1996) requires that:

- Religious Education in community and voluntary controlled schools must be provided for all registered pupils in accordance with the local agreed syllabus.
- every agreed syllabus shall reflect the fact that the religious traditions in Britain are, in the main, Christian while taking account of the teaching and practices of other principal religions represented in Britain.
- the local education authority and the governing body shall exercise their functions with a view to securing, and the head teacher shall secure, that the Religious Education is given in accordance with the agreed syllabus.
- parents have the right to request the withdrawal of their child from part of or all Religious Education.
- teachers have the right to withdraw from teaching the subject.
- Religious Education in special schools shall be taught, as far as is practicable, in accordance with the agreed syllabus.
- in a voluntary controlled school, if the parent requests it, arrangements must be made for Religious Education to be given to their child in accordance with any trust deed or the practice followed before the school became controlled.

— Appendix 2 —

Connecting Spiritual, Moral, Social and Cultural education with RE

All schools should promote pupils' spiritual, moral, social and cultural (SMSC) development and prepare pupils suitably for life. Ofsted guides inspectors to gather evidence of the impact of the curriculum on developing aspects of the pupils' SMSC development.

Inspectors should consider the climate and ethos of the school and what effect this has on enabling pupils to grow and flourish, become confident individuals, and appreciate their own worth and that of others. In considering how well the school promotes pupils' SMSC, inspectors should take into account the impact of the range of opportunities provided for young people to develop their self-esteem and confidence, which might occur both within the classroom, in terms of: teaching that encourages participation, creativity, reflection and independence; assessment and feedback that values pupils' work and/or effort; and activities that develop teamwork, leadership skills and self-reliance.

OFSTED SUBSIDIARY GUIDANCE DOCUMENT, PARAGRAPH 86

This information may be gathered through:

- lesson observations where subjects promote aspects of SMSC provision. RE, art and music are obvious examples but discussion with pupils and staff will provide an important insight into the way SMSC is planned as part of the curriculum in other subjects.
- observation of other activities that indicate the extent to which there is a coherent approach to promoting SMSC set out by the school and implemented through activities such as tutorials,

citizenship programmes and discussions with pupils about their work.
• evaluation of opportunities created by the school for pupils to take part in a range of artistic, cultural, sporting, dramatic, musical, mathematical, scientific, technological and, where appropriate, international events and activities that promote aspects of pupils' SMSC development.

Defining spiritual, moral, social and cultural development

The left-hand column in the table below indicates the Ofsted definition of each aspect of development (from the *Subsidiary Guidance* document, paragraph 86), while the right-hand column offers suggestions of ways in which it may be evidenced in RE.

Ofsted definition	RE evidence
Pupils' spiritual development is shown by their:	
Beliefs, religious or otherwise, which inform their perspective on life and their interest in and respect for different people's feelings and values.	**Year 6** role play situation: a church has £2000 to give away. Groups have to decide whether it is to go to the local donkey sanctuary, the children's hospice, a local homeless people's charity or a charity that is helping to feed people in another country who currently have no food. A charity is researched and arguments for and against the money allocation given. A class vote determines the distribution at the end.

Sense of enjoyment and fascination in learning about themselves, others and the world around them, including the intangible.	**Year 4** consider what is most fascinating about the world around them. They look for animals in Psalm 104 and, using a pattern for a psalm, write their own psalm of praise. **Year 5** investigate possible answers to the question 'What do you think happens when you die?' and create a presentation in any form (for example, PowerPoint, drama or collage) to the rest of the class.
Use of imagination and creativity in their learning.	**Year 3** make up their own creation story. **Year 4** design an altar frontal for a season of the year, using Christian symbols intertwined with the symbols representing the local community.
Willingness to reflect on their experiences.	**Year 4** compare a visit to a cathedral with a visit to a local church and consider which would be the place where they would choose to worship, if they were a Christian, and why.
Pupils' moral development is shown by their:	
Ability to recognise the difference between right and wrong and their readiness to apply this understanding in their own lives.	**Year 4** discuss good rules and bad rules. They look at the ten commandments and decide which rules are positive and which are negative. Which do they think is most important for a Christian? Which rule do they think is most important for a group of people living in a village?
Understanding of the consequences of their actions.	**Year 1** act out the parable of the lost sheep (Luke 15:1–7) using only ten sheep. At the final count of nine, the teacher asks: 'What will the shepherd do now? Why?'

Interest in investigating, and offering reasoned views about, moral and ethical issues.	**Year 1** use a Philosophy for Children approach to ask questions about what is right and what is wrong in the parable of the good Samaritan (Luke 10:25–37).
Pupils' social development is shown by their:	
Use of a range of social skills in different contexts, including working and socialising with pupils from different religious, ethnic and socio-economic backgrounds.	**Year 2**, in pairs, create their own questions to ask a Muslim visitor about a mosque and compare them with other generated questions to a Christian about a church.
Willingness to participate in a variety of social settings, cooperating well with others and being able to resolve conflicts effectively.	**Year 5** visit a Hindu temple, remove their shoes and ask questions about the *murtis*.
Interest in, and understanding of, the way communities and societies function at a variety of levels.	**Year 3** look at Christians in another country and the music they play compared with the music in their own school or in their local church.
Pupils' cultural development is shown by their:	
Understanding and appreciation of the wide range of cultural influences that have shaped their own heritage.	**Year 6** compare three faith communities in their locality (or wider) and interview members of the faith communities to find out how each contributes to the city/town.
Willingness to participate in and respond to (for example) artistic, musical, sporting, mathematical, technological, scientific and cultural opportunities.	**Year 3** learn some Indian dance movements and then create a dance to tell the story of Rama and Sita.

Interest in exploring, understanding of and respect for cultural diversity and the extent to which they understand, accept, respect and celebrate diversity, as shown by their attitudes towards different religious, ethnic and socio-economic groups in the local, national and global communities.	**Year 6** interview three Muslims or an Anglican, Roman Catholic and Baptist, to understand how the same religion might differ in practice.

— Appendix 3 —

Sample lesson observation form

Teacher:	Date:
Observer:	Class:
Subject:	Time:
Number of children:	Teacher support:
Number of children with statements:	Individual education plans:

Engage

The teacher engages the child by connecting the learning objective with the child's experience or offers an experience within the classroom to 'hook' the children—for example, a mystery bag with an artefact or object inside.

- Well-organised, tidy room, stimulating and conducive to learning
- Inclusive learning strategies
- Seating arrangement that supports learning
- Appropriate behaviour management
- Positive relationships

Enquire

The teacher's key questions or the child's questions help the children to engage at a deeper level with the material/content offered and to consider how to explore it.

- Questioning
- Modelling
- Explaining
- Thinking skills
- Literacy
- Activities
- Standards of presentation

Express

The children make their own responses to the story/questions/lesson content by offering their own interpretation.

- Extended concentration
- Children can explain what they are doing

Evaluate

The children evaluate and reflect on their learning, making meaningful links to their own lives.

— Appendix 4 —

More about the solid–liquid–gas analogy in enquiry learning

Ian Patience (www.thinkwell.org.uk) writes:

Lois Hetland and Kimberly Sheridan first used the 'solid–liquid–gas' states of matter metaphor in their work with art education students, to describe and qualitatively assess levels of learning in the visual arts across four aspects of learning: thinking, knowledge handling, evaluation and motivation. The structure was published in their book *Studio Thinking: The real benefits of visual arts education* by L. Hetland, E. Winner, S. Veenema and K. Sheridan (Teachers College Press, 2007).

Early in their development, art students may use knowledge in 'discrete', unconnected ways. Their thinking might be restricted to familiar, safe paths, their judgements of quality might stay within well-established boundaries of taste and they might rely on external sources of motivation to act and learn. By analogy, this phase of learning can be described as a 'solid' phase.

As they become more experienced, students begin to escape this 'rigid' state. Their thinking becomes more 'fluid' and receptive to new ideas. Categories of knowledge merge and interact, judgements are less bounded and their work begins to 'flow'—the 'liquid' phase.

At the most developed level, the 'gaseous' phase, their thinking is quick, interactive and responsive, knowledge is tacit, judgements are intuitive and the artwork seems to have a momentum of its own.

Hetland and Sheridan found the 'solid–liquid–gas' analogy, in combination with the four continua of growth, a useful diagnostic and formative assessment tool because it simplified the task of describing stages of development and identifying next steps.

We saw the potential for applying the analogy more generally, recognising that enquiry learning in the classroom can usefully happen within tightly controlled constraints, which become progressively more relaxed as students and teachers become more proficient with the tools and methods that support this way of learning.

As in art education, student enquirers grow through stages of development towards independence, as do teachers in their professional development of the qualities and skills that enable them to support independent enquiry.

The 'states of matter' metaphor allowed teachers and students to identify and discuss their current position on the solid–liquid–gas continuum so that the degree of structure and support provided in learning experiences could be determined to meet their needs.

*

References and sources

- Jane Brooke, *Where to Start with a Bible Story* (Chester Diocese), available from www.chester.anglican.org: go to 'Schools' tab, then 'RE and Worship' and 'RE'.
- Margaret Cooling, *More Bible Storybags* (Barnabas in Schools, 2012).
- Trevor Cooling, *Concept Cracking: Exploring Christian beliefs in schools* (Stapleford Centre, 1994).

- Information about P4C from www.p4c.com/about-p4c
- *Assessment for Learning: 10 Principles (Research-based principles to guide classroom practice)*: www.aaia.org.uk/content/uploads/2010/06/Assessment-for-Learning-10-principles.pdf

- For Ofsted guidance on Spiritual, Moral, Social and Cultural development, download the following documents:

  ❖ www.retoday.org.uk/media/display/Subsidiary_guidance.doc (complete document)
  ❖ www.retoday.org.uk/media/display/Extracts_from_Subsidiary_Guidance_issued_to_inspectors_January_2012.doc (key sections)

NB: All web links in this book are correct at time of going to press.

*

About the author

Jane Brooke has over 20 years' RE teaching experience and has taught pupils aged 3 to 18 years. She worked for CEM (now RE Today Services) for five years and in local authorities for over ten years as RE Adviser, Senior Curriculum Adviser and Principal Secondary Improvement Adviser. Jane was Chair of NASACRE for two years and the English representative on EFTRE (European Forum for Teachers of Religious Education) for nine years. She was RE Project Development Officer for three years for the National Society. She has led RE INSET nationally and internationally and is currently an independent consultant working for schools and local authorities as a School Improvement Partner and for Chester Diocese, where she is a Canon, as Principal Consultant. She is a project manager for the RE Quality Mark and a sub-editor for *RE Today*.